# Excel® 2016
# The VLOOKUP Formula
# in *30 Minutes* The
# Step-By-Step Guide

C.J. Benton

ISBN-13: 978-1979591621
ISBN-10: 1979591628

# Thank you!

Thank you for purchasing and reading this book! **Your feedback is valued and appreciated**. Please take a few minutes and leave a review.

# Other Books Available From This Author:

1. Microsoft® Excel® **Start Here The Beginners Guide**

2. The Step-By-Step Guide To The **25 Most Common Microsoft® Excel® Formulas & Features** (version **2013**)

3. The Excel® 2016 **The 30 Most Common Formulas & Features** - The Step-By-Step Guide (version **2016**)

4. The Step-By-Step Guide To **Pivot Tables & Introduction To Dashboards** (version **2013**)

5. **Excel® Pivot Tables & Introduction To Dashboards** The Step-By-Step Guide (version **2016**)

6. The Step-By-Step Guide To The **VLOOKUP** formula in Microsoft® Excel® (version **2013**)

7. The Microsoft® Excel® Step-By-Step Training Guide **Book Bundle** (version **2013**)

8. **Excel® Macros & VBA For Business Users** - A Beginners Guide

9. **Microsoft® Word® Essentials** The Step-By-Step Guide

# TABLE OF CONTENTS

This book can be used as a tutorial or quick reference guide. It is intended for users who are comfortable with the fundamentals of Microsoft® Excel® and want to build upon this skill by learning the very useful VLOOKUP functionality.

While this book is intended for beginners, it does assume you already know how to create, open, save, and modify an Excel® workbook and have a general familiarity with the Excel® Ribbon (toolbar).

All of the examples in this book use **Microsoft® Excel® 2016**, however most of the functionality can be applied with Microsoft® Excel® version 2013. All screenshots use **Microsoft® Excel® 2016**, functionality and display will be slightly different if using **Excel® 2013**.

Please always **back-up your work** and **save often**. A good best practice when attempting any new functionality is to **create a copy of the original spreadsheet** and implement your changes on the copied spreadsheet. Should anything go wrong, you then have the original spreadsheet to fall back on. Please see the diagram below.

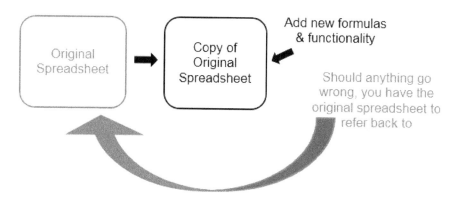

The below table is a summary of the functionality and features detailed in each chapter:

| CHAPTER | FUNCTIONALITY |
|---|---|
| **Chapter 2** <br> VLOOKUP Introduction | ▪ What the VLOOKUP formula does <br> ▪ The parts of a VLOOKUP formula <br> ▪ Two detailed examples with screenshots using a basic VLOOKUP formula |
| **Chapters 3 & 4** <br> Extending the Vlookup Functionality | ▪ Incorporating the IFERROR functionality into your VLOOKUP formula <br> ▪ What to do when you attempt to lookup a value in the Table_array, but none exists <br> ▪ What to do when you don't have a unique Lookup_value <br> ▪ What to do when the Lookup_value is listed more than once in the Table_array |
| **Chapter 5** <br> Using the VLOOKUP across tabs & workbooks | ▪ Detailed example with screenshots of how to apply the VLOOKUP formula across multiple workbooks and tabs <br> ▪ Detailed example with screenshots on how to use a VLOOKUP to lookup and calculate a number based on specific criteria |
| **Chapter 6** <br> VLOOKUP Troubleshooting | ▪ A review of five common VLOOKUP error messages / issues and how to resolve them |

## FILES FOR EXERCISES

The exercise files used in this book are available for download at the following website:

https://bentontrainingbook.wixsite.com/bentonbooks/excel-2016

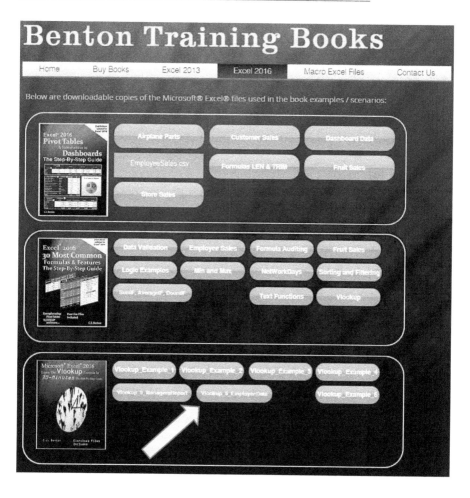

The VLOOKUP formula allows you to vertically search for a value from one Excel® list, and return that specific value to a new Excel® list, based on a *matching lookup value*.

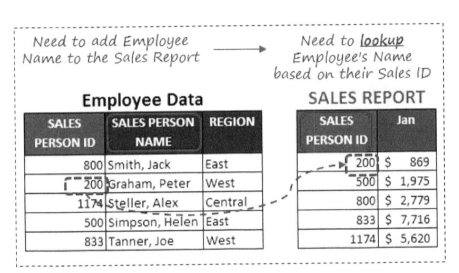

**Example:**

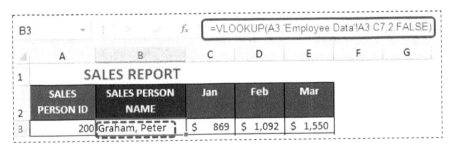

## THE 4 - PARTS OF A VLOOKUP

❶ **lookup value:**

This is the field you want to find (match) typically located on another worksheet (tab) or workbook.

In the example below, '**A2**' is selected, which has the Sales Person ID value of '**200**'. We will look to match this value on the tab labeled '**Sheet2**'. Sales Person Name is the value we want to lookup and be returned to the tab labeled '**Sheet1**'.

❷ **Table array:**

This is the spreadsheet (tab) and range of cells searched for the ❶ Lookup_value. The field you want to match <u>must be</u> in the <u>first column</u> of the range of cells you specify in the ❷ Table_array.

In the example below, I'm searching the tab labeled '**Sheet2**' with the cell range of '**A2:B6**'. The Lookup_value must be in **column 'A'**.

❸ **Col index num:**

Is the column containing the value you want returned. In the example below, column '**2**' of the tab labeled '**Sheet2**' contains value of Sales Person Name which we want returned to the tab labeled '**Sheet1**'.

❹ **Range lookup:**

Is the optional value of '**TRUE**' or '**FALSE**'. The value of '**FALSE**' would return an exact match, while '**TRUE**' would return an approximate match. Most often users enter '**FALSE**' for this parameter.

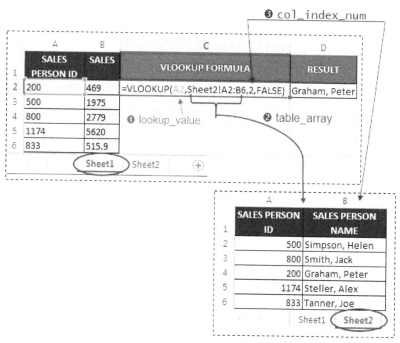

5

## Scenario:
You've been asked to provide a list of the first quarter sales by month for each sales person. You run a query from the sales database and generate an Excel® report. Unfortunately, the database only contains the sales person's ID, *but not their name.* You use a VLOOKUP formula to return the Sales Person's Name from an existing Excel® spreadsheet to the new sales report.

**WEB ADDRESS & FILE NAME FOR EXERCISE:**
https://bentontrainingbook.wixsite.com/bentonbooks/excel-2016
Vlookup_Example_1.xlsx

**Step-By-Step Example:**
EXAMPLE 1: (HOW-TO-CREATE A BASIC VLOOKUP FUNCTION)

Sample data:

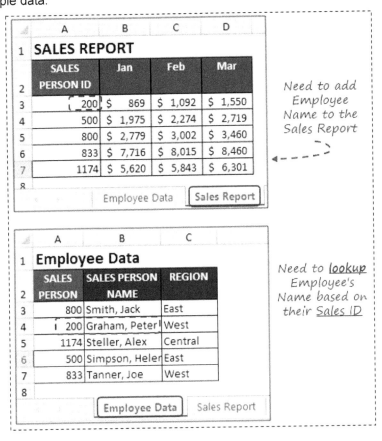

1. Open the Vlookup Example 1.xlsx spreadsheet

2. Select the tab named **'Sales Report'**

3. Place your cursor in cell **'B3'**

4. From the Ribbon select **Formulas : Lookup & Reference**

5. From the drop-down list, select the option **'VLOOKUP'**

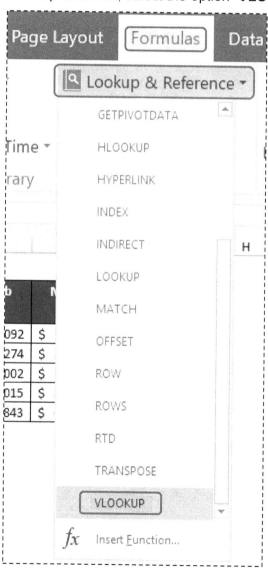

6. In the Function Arguments dialogue box enter the following:

a. Click cell '**A3**' or enter **A3** in the dialogue box for the '**Lookup_value**' *(the sales person ID is the field we'll lookup on the 'Employee Data' tab)*

b. For '**Table_array**', click on the tab '**Employee Data**' and select cells '**A3:C7**' *(this is the range of cells we're searching)*

c. Enter the number **2** for '**Col_index_num**' *(this is the column containing the sales person's name)*

d. For '**Range_lookup**' enter **FALSE**

7. Click the '**OK**' button

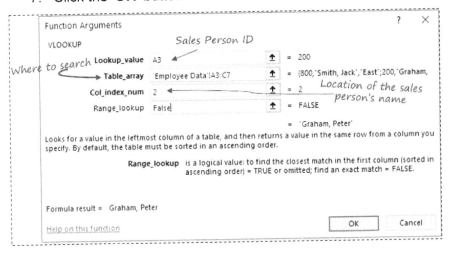

The following result should now be displayed on the **Sales Report** worksheet:

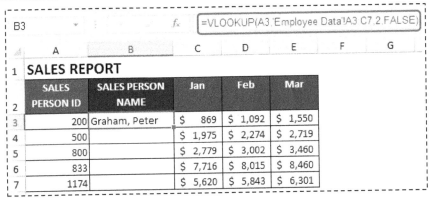

| | | | | | |
|---|---|---|---|---|---|
| **B3** | | $f_x$ | =VLOOKUP(A3,'Employee Data'!A3:C7,2,FALSE) | | |

| | A | B | C | D | E | F | G |
|---|---|---|---|---|---|---|---|
| 1 | **SALES REPORT** | | | | | | |
| 2 | **SALES PERSON ID** | **SALES PERSON NAME** | **Jan** | **Feb** | **Mar** | | |
| 3 | 200 | Graham, Peter | $ 869 | $ 1,092 | $ 1,550 | | |
| 4 | 500 | | $ 1,975 | $ 2,274 | $ 2,719 | | |
| 5 | 800 | | $ 2,779 | $ 3,002 | $ 3,460 | | |
| 6 | 833 | | $ 7,716 | $ 8,015 | $ 8,460 | | |
| 7 | 1174 | | $ 5,620 | $ 5,843 | $ 6,301 | | |

8. We need to do one additional step before we can copy this formula down to cells '**B4:B7**', we must add the U.S. dollar symbol **$** to the '**Table_array**'. This will prevent our cell range *(Table_array)* from changing:

↓↓ ↓↓

=VLOOKUP(A3,'Employee Data'**!$A$3:$C$7**,2,FALSE)

If we attempted to copy the VLOOKUP formula to cells '**B4:B7**' without adding the **$**, the result would be as follows, **NOTE:** *how the 'Table_array' cell range changes:*

| | A | B |
|---|---|---|
| 1 | **SALES REPORT** | |
| 2 | **SALES PERSO** | **SALES PERSON NAME** |
| 3 | 200 | =VLOOKUP(A3,'Employee Data'!A3:C7,2,FALSE) |
| 4 | 500 | =VLOOKUP(A4,'Employee Data'!A4:C8,2,FALSE) |
| 5 | 800 | =VLOOKUP(A5,'Employee Data'!A5:C9,2,FALSE) |
| 6 | 833 | =VLOOKUP(A6,'Employee Data'!A6:C10,2,FALSE) |
| 7 | 1174 | =VLOOKUP(A7,'Employee Data'!A7:C11,2,FALSE) |

*Table_array changes*

We would also receive a #N/A error in cells '**B5**' & '**B7**'

| | A | B | C | D | E |
|---|---|---|---|---|---|
| 1 | **SALES REPORT** | | | | |
| 2 | **SALES PERSON ID** | **SALES PERSON NAME** | **Jan** | **Feb** | **Mar** |
| 3 | 200 | Graham, Peter | $ 869 | $ 1,092 | $ 1,550 |
| 4 | 500 | Simpson, Helen | $ 1,975 | $ 2,274 | $ 2,719 |
| 5 | 800 | #N/A | $ 2,779 | $ 3,002 | $ 3,460 |
| 6 | 833 | Tanner, Joe | $ 7,716 | $ 8,015 | $ 8,460 |
| 7 | 1174 | #N/A | $ 5,620 | $ 5,843 | $ 6,301 |

9. Copy the VLOOKUP formula to cells '**B4:B7**'

=VLOOKUP(A3,'Employee Data'**!$A$3:$C$7**,2,FALSE)

9

| ⬜ | A | B | C | D | E |
|---|---|---|---|---|---|
| 1 | **SALES REPORT** | | | | |
| 2 | SALES PERSON ID | SALES PERSON NAME | Jan | Feb | Mar |
| 3 | 200 | Graham, Peter | $ 869 | $ 1,092 | $ 1,550 |
| 4 | 500 | Simpson, Helen | $ 1,975 | $ 2,274 | $ 2,719 |
| 5 | 800 | Smith, Jack | $ 2,779 | $ 3,002 | $ 3,460 |
| 6 | 833 | Tanner, Joe | $ 7,716 | $ 8,015 | $ 8,460 |
| 7 | 1174 | Steller, Alex | $ 5,620 | $ 5,843 | $ 6,301 |

| ⬜ | A | B | C | D | E |
|---|---|---|---|---|---|
| 1 | SALES REPORT | | | | |
| 2 | SALES PERSON ID | SALES PERSON NAME | Jan | Feb | Mar |
| 3 | 200 | =VLOOKUP(A3,'Employee Data'!$A$3:$C$7,2,FALSE) | 869 | 1092 | 1550 |
| 4 | 500 | =VLOOKUP(A4,'Employee Data'!$A$3:$C$7,2,FALSE) | 1975 | 2274 | 2719 |
| 5 | 800 | =VLOOKUP(A5,'Employee Data'!$A$3:$C$7,2,FALSE) | 2779 | 3002 | 3460 |
| 6 | 833 | =VLOOKUP(A6,'Employee Data'!$A$3:$C$7,2,FALSE) | 7715.9 | 8014.9 | 8459.9 |
| 7 | 1174 | =VLOOKUP(A7,'Employee Data'!$A$3:$C$7,2,FALSE) | 5620 | 5843 | 6301 |

We have successfully looked-up and added the Sales Person Name to the quarterly sales report. We can now provide a list of the first quarter sales by month for each sales person.

Alternatively, for the **'Table_array'**, instead entering the range of cells (Employee Data!$A$3:$C$7) and having to add the $ to hold the array constant, you may enter the entire column **A:C** (Employee Data !A:C), provided the *entire column* contains the data you want returned. This would eliminate the need to complete **step 8**. However, depending on the number of records you're looking up *(the size of your data)*, there could be a reduction in performance speed when selecting the entire column. Especially, when using multiple functions together, for example combining a Nested IF and

VLOOKUP. Please see the below screenshots for a complete example using entire columns instead of cell ranges:

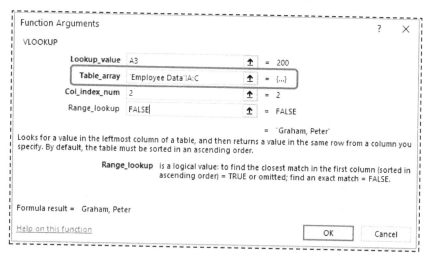

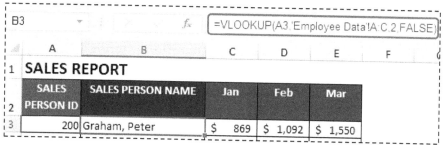

## Scenario:

You've now been asked to include the **sales region** to the list of the first quarter sales by month, for each sales person.

**WEB ADDRESS & FILE NAME FOR EXERCISE:**
https://bentontrainingbook.wixsite.com/bentonbooks/excel-2016
Vlookup_Example_2.xlsx

**Step-By-Step Example:**

## EXAMPLE 2: (HOW-TO-APPLY A VLOOKUP USING THE ENTIRE COLUMN)

Sample data:

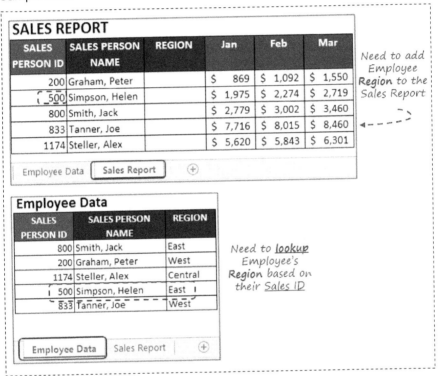

1. Open the Vlookup_Example_2.xlsx spreadsheet
2. Select the tab named '**Sales Report**'

3. Place your cursor in cell '**C3**'
4. From the Ribbon select **Formulas : Lookup & Reference**
5. From the drop-down list, select the option '**VLOOKUP**'

In the Function Arguments dialogue box enter the following:

   a.   Click cell '**A3**' or enter **A3** in the dialogue box for the '**Lookup_value**' *(the sales person ID is the field we'll lookup on the 'Employee Data' tab)*

   b.   For '**Table_array**', click on the tab '**Employee Data**' and select columns '**A:C**' *(this is the range of cells we're searching)*

   c.   Enter the number **3** for '**Col_index_num**' *(this is the column containing the sales person's region)*

   d.   For '**Range_lookup**' enter **FALSE**

6.  Click the '**OK**' button

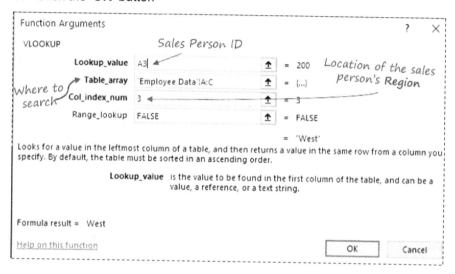

The following should be the result:

| C3 | | | | $f_x$ | =VLOOKUP(A3,'Employee Data'!A:C,3,FALSE) | |
|----|---|---|---|---|---|---|
| | A | B | C | D | E | F |
| 1 | **SALES REPORT** | | | | | |
| 2 | **SALES PERSON ID** | **SALES PERSON NAME** | **REGION** | **Jan** | **Feb** | **Mar** |
| 3 | 200 | Graham, Peter | West | $ 869 | $ 1,092 | $ 1,550 |
| 4 | 500 | Simpson, Helen | | $ 1,975 | $ 2,274 | $ 2,719 |
| 5 | 800 | Smith, Jack | | $ 2,779 | $ 3,002 | $ 3,460 |
| 6 | 833 | Tanner, Joe | | $ 7,716 | $ 8,015 | $ 8,460 |
| 7 | 1174 | Steller, Alex | | $ 5,620 | $ 5,843 | $ 6,301 |

7. Copy this formula down to cells '**C4:C7**'

The following should be the result:

| | A | B | C | D | E | F |
|---|---|---|---|---|---|---|
| | SALES PERS | SALES PERSON NAME | REGION | Jan | Feb | Mar |
| 1 | | | | | | |
| 2 | 200 | Graham, Peter | West | $ 869 | $ 1,092 | $ 1,550 |
| 3 | 500 | Simpson, Helen | East | $ 1,975 | $ 2,274 | $ 2,719 |
| 4 | 800 | Smith, Jack | East | $ 2,779 | $ 3,002 | $ 3,460 |
| 5 | 833 | Tanner, Joe | West | $ 7,716 | $ 8,015 | $ 8,460 |
| 6 | 1174 | Steller, Alex | Central | $ 5,620 | $ 5,843 | $ 6,301 |

We have successfully looked-up and added the Sales Person's **Region** to the quarterly sales report.

# PUBLISHING VLOOKUP RESULTS

When sending the results of a VLOOKUP function to a customer or a co-worker, a common mistake beginners often make is including the VLOOKUP formula in the spreadsheet, rather than pasting the results as a value. This is a very easy thing to do, but depending on where the **Table_array** worksheet or workbook is located can cause the following to happen.

Let's say in the example above, after adding the Sales Person Name & Region you deleted the worksheet, '**Employee Data**', because you no longer needed the information.

- You saved the workbook without noticing the VLOOKUP function is now broken.
- You emailed the spreadsheet results to a customer.
- When they open the spreadsheet, they likely would see an error in the results:

# SALES REPORT

| SALES PERSON ID | SALES PERSON NAME | REGION | Jan | Feb | Mar |
|---|---|---|---|---|---|
| 200 | #REF! | #REF! | $ 869 | $ 1,092 | $ 1,550 |
| 500 | #REF! | #REF! | $ 1,975 | $ 2,274 | $ 2,719 |
| 800 | #REF! | #REF! | $ 2,779 | $ 3,002 | $ 3,460 |
| 833 | #REF! | #REF! | $ 7,716 | $ 8,015 | $ 8,460 |
| 1174 | #REF! | #REF! | $ 5,620 | $ 5,843 | $ 6,301 |

Another common scenario, if the **Table_array** was located in a *separate workbook*.

- You saved the workbook without issue
- You emailed the spreadsheet results to a co-worker
- When they open the spreadsheet, they likely would see a **!SECURITY WARING** message about the *file being linked to another workbook*:

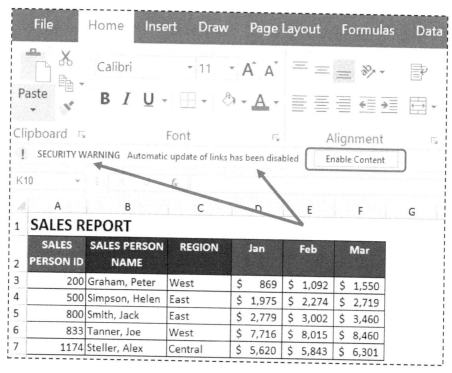

- If they clicked the **'Enable Content'** button, they may receive the following message:

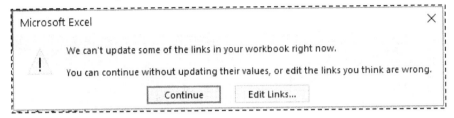

In either scenario, it could cause confusion, rework, or even lead a customer to have questions about you or the company you represent.

One of the easiest ways to address this issue is to **simply paste your VLOOKUP results as a value**. In the example above, we would:

1. Select (highlight) cells '**B3:C7**'
2. Click the '**Copy**' button or press **CTL+C** from your keyboard
3. From the '**Paste**' drop-down menu select **'Paste Values'**
4. Select the **'123'** option

*Please see image on next page:*

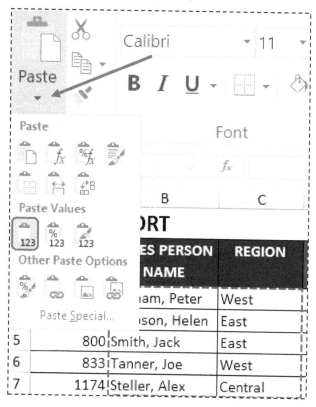

The VLOOKUP results are intact without any risk of error when you send them to a customer or a co-worker.

In this chapter we examine what to do when you attempt to lookup a value in the **Table_array**, but the value does not exist. Specifically, how to handle receiving the #N/A error message in your result set.

Before continuing, we must quickly review three functions needed to extend the VLOOKUP functionality. If you're already familiar with the **IF**, **Nested IF**, & **IFERROR** formulas, please continue to the section Addressing Error Messages, page 19.

| FUNCTION | DEFINITION |
|---|---|
| IF | IF formulas allow you test conditions and return one value *if true* and another *if false* |
| NESTED IF | NESTED IF formulas allow you test conditions and return one value *if true* and another *if false*, if certain criteria is met* |
| IFERROR | IFERROR returns a value you specify if a function *(in our case the VLOOKUP formula)* evaluates an error such as: #N/A, #VALUE!, #REF!, #DIV/0!, #NUM!, #NAME?, or #NULL! *Otherwise* IFERROR will return the result of the *(VLOOKUP)* formula |

**Examples:**

```
IF Syntax:
IF(logical_test, value_if_true, [value_if_false])
logic_test required, value_if_true required,
value_if_false optional
```

*Basic IF formula:*

| F2 | ▼ | : | ✕ | ✓ | *fx* | =IF(B2=D2,"Pass","Fail") |

| | A | B | C | D | E | F |
|---|---|---|---|---|---|---|
| 1 | **RESULTS 1** | **COUNT** | **RESULTS 2** | **COUNT** | | **If results match, indicate with the word "Pass"** |
| 2 | Test #1 | 111 | Test #1 | 111 | | Pass ← |
| 3 | Test #2 | 161 | Test #2 | 158 | | Fail |

*Nested IF formula:*

| F4 | ▼ | : | ✕ | ✓ | *fx* | =IF(B4=D4,"Pass",IF(B4-D4>5,"BIG FAIL","Fail")) |

| | A | B | C | D | E | F |
|---|---|---|---|---|---|---|
| 1 | **RESULTS 1** | **COUNT** | **RESULTS 2** | **COUNT** | | IF results match = **Pass**<br>IF results DO NOT match = **Fail**<br>IF results DO NOT match and the difference is greater than 5 = **BIG FAIL** |
| 2 | Test #1 | 111 | Test #1 | 111 | | Pass |
| 3 | Test #2 | 161 | Test #2 | 158 | | Fail |
| 4 | Test #3 | 183 | Test #3 | 175 | | BIG FAIL ← |
| 5 | Test #4 | 243 | Test #4 | 243 | | Pass |
| 6 | Test #5 | 263 | Test #5 | 260 | | Fail |

```
IFERROR Syntax:
IFERROR(value, value_if_error)
All parameters are required
```

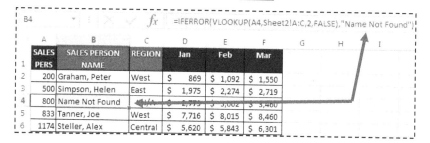

| B4 | ▼ | : | ✕ | ✓ | *fx* | =IFERROR(VLOOKUP(A4,Sheet2!A:C,2,FALSE),"Name Not Found") |

| | A | B | C | D | E | F | G | H | I |
|---|---|---|---|---|---|---|---|---|---|
| 1 | **SALES PERS** | **SALES PERSON NAME** | **REGION** | **Jan** | **Feb** | **Mar** | | | |
| 2 | 200 | Graham, Peter | West | $ 869 | $ 1,092 | $ 1,550 | | | |
| 3 | 500 | Simpson, Helen | East | $ 1,975 | $ 2,274 | $ 2,719 | | | |
| 4 | 800 | Name Not Found | N/A | $ 2,773 | $ 3,002 | $ 3,460 | | | |
| 5 | 833 | Tanner, Joe | West | $ 7,716 | $ 8,015 | $ 8,460 | | | |
| 6 | 1174 | Steller, Alex | Central | $ 5,620 | $ 5,843 | $ 6,301 | | | |

# ADDRESSING ERROR MESSAGES

## Scenario:

You've been asked to provide a list of first quarter sales by month, for each sales person. However, *if* the Sales Person's name is not available, display the text "**Name Not Found.**" To accomplish this, you use a combination of formulas **IFERROR** & **VLOOKUP** to develop the sales report.

WEB ADDRESS & FILE NAME FOR EXERCISE:
https://bentontrainingbook.wixsite.com/bentonbooks/excel-2016
Vlookup_Example_3.xlsx

**Step-By-Step Example:**

EXAMPLE 3: (IFERROR AND THE VLOOKUP)

Sample data:

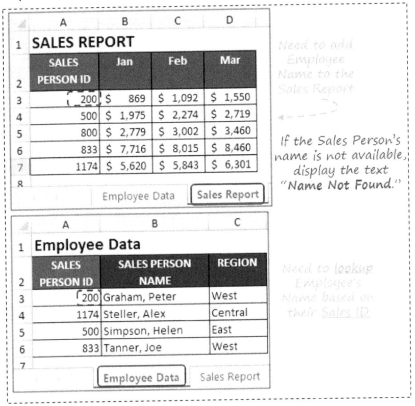

1. Open the Vlookup_Example_3.xlsx spreadsheet

2. Select the tab named '**Sales Report**'

3. Place your cursor in cell **'B3'**

4. From the Ribbon select **Formulas : Lookup & Reference**

5. From the drop-down list, select the option **'VLOOKUP'**

6. In the Function Arguments dialogue box enter the following:

   a. Click cell '**A3**' or enter **A3** in the dialogue box for the **'Lookup_value'**

   b. For **'Table_array'**, click on the tab **'Employee Data'** and select **columns 'A:C'**

   c. Enter the number **2** for '**Col_index_num**'

   d. For **'Range_lookup'** enter **False**

7. Click the '**OK**' button

The following result should now be displayed on the **Sales Report** worksheet:

| B3 | | | | $f_x$ | =VLOOKUP(A3,'Employee Data'!A3:C7,2,FALSE) | |
|---|---|---|---|---|---|---|
| | A | B | C | D | E | F | G |
| 1 | SALES REPORT | | | | | | |
| 2 | SALES PERSON ID | SALES PERSON NAME | Jan | Feb | Mar | | |
| 3 | 200 | Graham, Peter | $ 869 | $ 1,092 | $ 1,550 | | |
| 4 | 500 | | $ 1,975 | $ 2,274 | $ 2,719 | | |
| 5 | 800 | | $ 2,779 | $ 3,002 | $ 3,460 | | |
| 6 | 833 | | $ 7,716 | $ 8,015 | $ 8,460 | | |
| 7 | 1174 | | $ 5,620 | $ 5,843 | $ 6,301 | | |

8. Copy the formula down to cells '**B4:B7**'

The following should be the result. *Note:* the error *#N/A* in cell '*B5*', this occurs because in the **Table_array (Employee Data)** there is no Sales Person ID for *ID# 800*

21

| A | B | C | D | E |
|---|---|---|---|---|
| **1 SALES REPORT** | | | | |
| **2 SALES PERSON ID** | **SALES PERSON NAME** | **Jan** | **Feb** | **Mar** |
| 3 200 | Graham, Peter | $ 869 | $ 1,092 | $ 1,550 |
| 4 500 | Simpson, Helen | $ 1,975 | $ 2,274 | $ 2,719 |
| 5 800 | #N/A | $ 2,779 | $ 3,002 | $ 3,460 |
| 6 833 | Tanner, Joe | $ 7,716 | $ 8,015 | $ 8,460 |
| 7 1174 | Steller, Alex | $ 5,620 | $ 5,843 | $ 6,301 |

We were asked to provide a list of first quarter sales by month, for each sales person. However, *if* the Sales Person's name is not available, display the text **"Name Not Found."** To address this requirement we will add the function **IFERROR** to our **VLOOKUP** formula.

9. Select cell **'B3'** on the worksheet **'Sales Report'**

10. Add the **IFERROR** formula to the existing **VLOOKUP** function as follows:

```
=IFERROR(VLOOKUP(A3,'Employee Data'!A:C,2,FALSE),"Name Not Found")
```

The following should be the result:

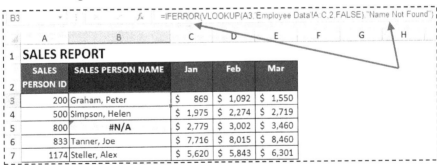

11. Copy this formula down to cells **'B4:B7'**

**Note:** the previous error of **#N/A** in cell '**B5**' is removed and now displays "**Name Not Found**"

| | A | B | C | D | E |
|---|---|---|---|---|---|
| 1 | **SALES REPORT** | | | | |
| 2 | **SALES PERSON ID** | **SALES PERSON NAME** | **Jan** | **Feb** | **Mar** |
| 3 | 200 | Graham, Peter | $ 869 | $ 1,092 | $ 1,550 |
| 4 | 500 | Simpson, Helen | $ 1,975 | $ 2,274 | $ 2,719 |
| 5 | 800 | **Name Not Found** | $ 2,779 | $ 3,002 | $ 3,460 |
| 6 | 833 | Tanner, Joe | $ 7,716 | $ 8,015 | $ 8,460 |
| 7 | 1174 | Steller, Alex | $ 5,620 | $ 5,843 | $ 6,301 |

You've now created a list of first quarter sales by month, for each sales person and when the Sales Person's name is unavailable, the text **"Name Not Found"** is displayed.

---

☑ **HELPFUL INFORMATION:**

The **IF**ERROR formula was introduced in Microsoft® Excel® version 2007, prior to this, many of us would use **IS**ERROR. I include an example of **IS**ERROR in this book, because I still see many people use this function in spreadsheets today. In the exercise above, someone may use the **IS**ERROR formula to accomplish the same thing as **IFERROR**, below is an example of the how the formula would be written:

```
=IF(ISERROR(VLOOKUP(A5,'Employee Data'!A:C,2,FALSE)),
"Name Not Found",(VLOOKUP(A5,'Employee Data'!A:C,2,FALSE)))
```

*Please see image on next page:*

| B5 | | | $f_x$ | =IF(ISERROR(VLOOKUP(A5,'Employee Data'!A:C,2,FALSE)),"Name Not Found", (VLOOKUP(A5,'Employee Data'!A:C,2,FALSE))) | | | | | |
|---|---|---|---|---|---|---|---|---|---|

| | A | B | C | D | E | F | G | H | I |
|---|---|---|---|---|---|---|---|---|---|
| 1 | **SALES REPORT** | | | | | | | | |
| 2 | SALES PERSON ID | SALES PERSON NAME | Jan | Feb | Mar | | | | |
| 3 | 200 | Graham, Peter | $ 869 | $ 1,092 | $ 1,550 | | | | |
| 4 | 500 | Simpson, Helen | $ 1,975 | $ 2,274 | $ 2,719 | | | | |
| 5 | 800 | **Name Not Found** | $ 2,779 | $ 3,002 | $ 3,460 | | | | |
| 6 | 833 | Tanner, Joe | $ 7,716 | $ 8,015 | $ 8,460 | | | | |
| 7 | 1174 | Steller, Alex | $ 5,620 | $ 5,843 | $ 6,301 | | | | |

As you can see, **IF**ERROR greatly simplifies this type of functionality.

This concludes the first part of the book, learning the basic

# Vlookup formula in 30 minutes

The following chapters are intended <u>when you have more time</u> and would like to extend the Vlookup functionality even further.

When time allows and you're ready to learn more about the power of the VLOOKUP the remaining chapters will guide you through how to manage some challenges that may arise when using the VLOOKUP formula such as:

- What to do when you don't have a unique **Lookup_value**
- When the **Lookup_value** is listed more than once in the **Table_array**

## WHEN YOU DON'T HAVE A UNIQUE LOOKUP_VALUE

Another common issue when using the VLOOKUP formula is occasionally you will *not* have a unique **Lookup_value**. In the previous examples, we used a unique sale person ID number. **What would we do if we only had a list of first and last names?** To tackle this question, we're going to introduce another function called **CONCAT** or CONCATENATE *(Excel® v2013 & earlier)*. Please skip this section if you're already familiar with concatenation.

| FUNCTION | DEFINITION |
|---|---|
| CONCAT / CONCATENATE | Joins two or more cells together, also allows the option to insert additional text into the merged cell |

**Example:**

| | A | B | C | D |
|---|---|---|---|---|
| 1 | SALES PERSON FIRST NAME | SALES PERSON LAST NAME | FORMULA | Merged cells 'B2' & 'A2', Last Name, followed by a comma and space, then First Name |
| 2 | Jack | Smith | =CONCATENATE(B2,", ",A2) | Smith, Jack |

| Function Syntax: | Function Syntax: | |
|---|---|---|
| CONCAT(text) | CONCATENATE(text) | *Excel version* |
| text is required | text is required | *2013 & earlier* |

Alternatively, you may perform the same type of functionality, by using the **ampersand (&) symbol**. This is how many intermediate and advanced Excel® users typically execute this command. Please see below for an example:

| C2 | | | $f_x$ | =A2&B2&"@fakecompany.com" |
|---|---|---|---|---|
| | A | B | | C |
| 1 | FIRST NAME | LAST NAME | | EMAIL ADDRESS |
| 2 | Billy | Winchester | | BillyWinchester@fakecompany.com |

## Scenario:

You've been given a list of employees and their first quarter sales, you need to lookup what sales region each employee belongs too. You attempt to use the VLOOKUP formula, however upon further review of the two files, you discover the sales report contains only the sales person's first and last name, *but not their sales person ID number.* Therefore, you're not sure what the unique **Lookup_value** should be. *You're unable to lookup based on first or last name alone, because more than one employee has either the same first or last name.* You decide to use the CONCAT function to create a unique **Lookup_value**.

WEB ADDRESS & FILE NAME FOR EXERCISE:
https://bentontrainingbook.wixsite.com/bentonbooks/excel-2016
Vlookup_Example_4.xlsx

## Step-By-Step Example:

### EXAMPLE 4: (COMBINING COLUMNS TO CREATE A UNIQUE LOOKUP_VALUE)

Sample data:

*Need to add Employee **Region** to the Sales Report*

| | A | B | C | D | E |
|---|---|---|---|---|---|
| | **SALES PERSON FIRST** | **SALES PERSON LAST** | **Jan** | **Feb** | **Mar** |
| 1 | | | | | |
| 2 | Peter | Danner | $ 4,449 | $ 7,048 | $ 5,746 |
| 3 | Maggie | Graham | $ 3,973 | $ 6,251 | $ 7,719 |
| 4 | Peter | Graham | $ 1,975 | $ 2,274 | $ 2,719 |
| 5 | Helen | Simpson | $ 7,716 | $ 8,015 | $ 8,460 |
| 6 | Alex | Steller | $ 2,779 | $ 3,002 | $ 3,460 |
| 7 | Joe | Tanner | $ 5,620 | $ 5,843 | $ 6,301 |
| 8 | Elizabeth | Winchester | $ 869 | $ 1,092 | $ 1,550 |
| 9 | | | | | |

Employee Data | Sales Report | ⊕

*No **Sales Person ID**, can't use **First** or **Last Name** as the Lookup_value, because more than one employee has either the same first or last name*

1. Open the Vlookup_Example_4.xlsx spreadsheet

2. Select the tab named **'Sales Report'**

3. Insert a column on the sales report before **'SALES PERSON FIRST'**
   A. Right-click the current **Column 'A'** *(SALES PERSON FIRST)*
   B. From the drop-down box select the option **'Insert'**

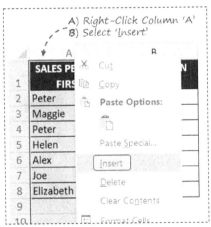

*A) Right-Click Column 'A'*
*B) Select 'Insert'*

4. Label the new **column 'A'**, cell **'A1'** as 'VLOOKUP ID' *(this column is going to become our new Lookup_value)*

The sales report should now look similar to the following:

| | A | B | C | D | E | F |
|---|---|---|---|---|---|---|
| | VLOOKUP ID | SALES PERSON FIRST | SALES PERSON LAST | Jan | Feb | Mar |
| 1 | | | | | | |
| 2 | | Peter | Danner | $ 4,449 | $ 7,048 | $ 5,746 |
| 3 | | Maggie | Graham | $ 3,973 | $ 6,251 | $ 7,719 |
| 4 | | Peter | Graham | $ 1,975 | $ 2,274 | $ 2,719 |
| 5 | | Helen | Simpson | $ 7,716 | $ 8,015 | $ 8,460 |
| 6 | | Alex | Steller | $ 2,779 | $ 3,002 | $ 3,460 |
| 7 | | Joe | Tanner | $ 5,620 | $ 5,843 | $ 6,301 |
| 8 | | Elizabeth | Winchester | $ 869 | $ 1,092 | $ 1,550 |

5. Place your cursor in cell **'A2'**

6. From the Ribbon select **Formulas : Text**

7. From the drop-down list, select the option **'CONCAT'**

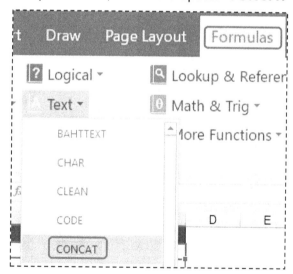

8. In the Function Arguments dialogue box enter the following:
   a. **Text1** box click cell 'C2' or enter **C2**
   b. **Text2** box enter a hyphen - *(dash or minus symbol)*
   c. **Text3** box enter the text 'B2' or enter **B2**

9. Click the '**OK**' button

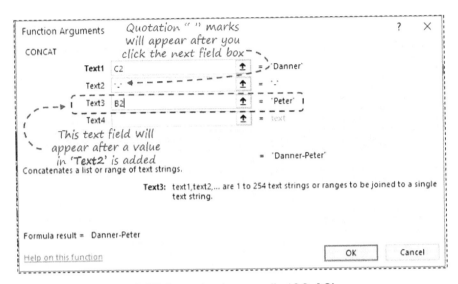

10. Copy the **CONCAT** formula down cells '**A3:A8**'

| | A | B | C | D | E | F |
|---|---|---|---|---|---|---|
| | | SALES PERSON | SALES PERSON | Jan | Feb | Mar |
| 1 | VLOOKUP ID | FIRST | LAST | | | |
| 2 | Danner-Peter | Peter | Danner | $ 4,449 | $ 7,048 | $ 5,746 |
| 3 | | Maggie | Graham | $ 3,973 | $ 6,251 | $ 7,719 |
| 4 | | Peter | Graham | $ 1,975 | $ 2,274 | $ 2,719 |
| 5 | | Helen | Simpson | $ 7,716 | $ 8,015 | $ 8,460 |
| 6 | | Alex | Steller | $ 2,779 | $ 3,002 | $ 3,460 |
| 7 | | Joe | Tanner | $ 5,620 | $ 5,843 | $ 6,301 |
| 8 | | Elizabeth | Winchester | $ 869 | $ 1,092 | $ 1,550 |

A2 = CONCAT(C2,"-",B2)

*Copy formula to cells 'A3:A8'*

11. Copy this formula to cells '**A3:A8**'

12. Press the '**Esc**' *(Escape)* button on your keyboard twice

13. Insert a column between columns '**C**' & '**D**'

| | A | B | C | D | E | F | G |
|---|---|---|---|---|---|---|---|
| | | SALES PERSON | SALES PERSON | | Jan | Feb | Mar |
| 1 | VLOOKUP ID | FIRST | LAST | REGION | | | |
| 2 | Danner-Peter | Peter | Danner | | $ 4,449 | $ 7,048 | $ 5,746 |
| 3 | Graham-Maggie | Maggie | Graham | | $ 3,973 | $ 6,251 | $ 7,719 |
| 4 | Graham-Peter | Peter | Graham | | $ 1,975 | $ 2,274 | $ 2,719 |
| 5 | Simpson-Helen | Helen | Simpson | | $ 7,716 | $ 8,015 | $ 8,460 |
| 6 | Steller-Alex | Alex | Steller | | $ 2,779 | $ 3,002 | $ 3,460 |
| 7 | Tanner-Joe | Joe | Tanner | | $ 5,620 | $ 5,843 | $ 6,301 |
| 8 | Winchester-Eliza | Elizabeth | Winchester | | $ 869 | $ 1,092 | $ 1,550 |

14. Label the new **column 'D'**, cell '**D1**' as '**REGION**'

## 15. Select the '**Employee Data**' worksheet

| | A | B | C | D | E |
|---|---|---|---|---|---|
| 1 | SALES PERSON ID | SALES PERSON LAST | SALES PERSON FIRST | SALES REGION | MANAGER ID |
| 2 | 100 | Winchester | Elizabeth | West | 50 |
| 3 | 200 | Graham | Peter | West | 50 |
| 4 | 300 | Steller | Alex | Central | 30 |
| 5 | 400 | Simpson | Helen | East | 40 |
| 6 | 500 | Tanner | Joe | West | 50 |
| 7 | 600 | Graham | Maggie | Central | 30 |
| 8 | 700 | Danner | Peter | East | 40 |

Employee Data | Sales Report | ⊕

16. Insert a column before '**SALES PERSON ID**'

17. Label the new **column 'A1'** as 'VLOOKUP ID'

18. In cell '**A2**' apply the following CONCAT formula:
=CONCAT(C2,"-",D2)

A2     *fx*    =CONCAT(C2,"-",D2)

| | A | B | C | D | E | F |
|---|---|---|---|---|---|---|
| 1 | VLOOKUP ID | SALES PERSON ID | SALES PERSON LAST | SALES PERSON FIRST | SALES REGION | MANAGER ID |
| 2 | Winchester-Elizabeth | 100 | Winchester | Elizabeth | West | 50 |
| 3 | | 200 | Graham | Peter | West | 50 |
| 4 | | 300 | Steller | Alex | Central | 30 |
| 5 | | 400 | Simpson | Helen | East | 40 |
| 6 | | 500 | Tanner | Joe | West | 50 |
| 7 | | 600 | Graham | Maggie | Central | 30 |
| 8 | | 700 | Danner | Peter | East | 40 |

19. Copy the CONCAT formula to cells '**A3:A8**'

20. Press the '**Esc**' *(Escape)* button on your keyboard twice

21. Return to the **Sales Report** worksheet

22. Select cell '**D2**' and apply the following VLOOKUP formula:

=VLOOKUP(A2,'Employee Data'!A:F,5,FALSE)

23. Copy VLOOKUP formula to cells '**D3:D8**'

| D2 | | $f_x$ | =VLOOKUP(A2,'Employee Data'!A:F,5,FALSE) | | | | |
|---|---|---|---|---|---|---|---|
| | A | B | C | D | E | F | G |
| 1 | VLOOKUP ID | SALES PERSON FIRST | SALES PERSON LAST | REGION | Jan | Feb | Mar |
| 2 | Danner-Peter | Peter | Danner | East | $ 4,449 | $ 7,048 | $ 5,746 |
| 3 | Graham-Maggie | Maggie | Graham | Central | $ 3,973 | $ 6,251 | $ 7,719 |
| 4 | Graham-Peter | Peter | Graham | West | $ 1,975 | $ 2,274 | $ 2,719 |
| 5 | Simpson-Helen | Helen | Simpson | East | $ 7,716 | $ 8,015 | $ 8,460 |
| 6 | Steller-Alex | Alex | Steller | Central | $ 2,779 | $ 3,002 | $ 3,460 |
| 7 | Tanner-Joe | Joe | Tanner | West | $ 5,620 | $ 5,843 | $ 6,301 |
| 8 | Winchester-Eliza| Elizabeth | Winchester | West | $ 869 | $ 1,092 | $ 1,550 |

24. Highlight cells '**D2:D8**' and click the '**Copy**' button or press **CTL+C** from your keyboard

25. From the '**Paste**' drop-down menu select '**Paste Values**' the '**123**' option (click here for an example)

26. After you **paste as a value**, you may delete **column 'A'** on the **Sales Report** worksheet

| | A | B | C | D | E | F |
|---|---|---|---|---|---|---|
| 1 | SALES PERSON FIRST | SALES PERSON LAST | REGION | Jan | Feb | Mar |
| 2 | Peter | Danner | East | $ 4,449 | $ 7,048 | $ 5,746 |
| 3 | Maggie | Graham | Central | $ 3,973 | $ 6,251 | $ 7,719 |
| 4 | Peter | Graham | West | $ 1,975 | $ 2,274 | $ 2,719 |
| 5 | Helen | Simpson | East | $ 7,716 | $ 8,015 | $ 8,460 |
| 6 | Alex | Steller | Central | $ 2,779 | $ 3,002 | $ 3,460 |
| 7 | Joe | Tanner | West | $ 5,620 | $ 5,843 | $ 6,301 |
| 8 | Elizabeth | Winchester | West | $ 869 | $ 1,092 | $ 1,550 |

You now have a list of employees, their first quarter sales results, and sales region.

---

☑ **HELPFUL INFORMATION:**

While the **CONCAT** function is helpful when you do not have a unique **Lookup_value** for your VLOOKUP formula, there are **risks** with this alternative. In the example above, if our data sample was larger, there would an increased probability of more than one person having the same first and last name combination. However, sometimes this can't be avoided, the risks are outweighed by the value the VLOOKUP brings to task efficiency.

The next section discusses the implications of what happens when you have the same **Lookup_value** listed more than once.

## WHEN A LOOKUP_VALUE IS LISTED MORE THAN ONCE IN THE TABLE_ARRAY

When the Lookup_value is listed more than once on the Table_array, the VLOOKUP function will always return the value for *the first* **matching Lookup_value it finds in the Table_array**. Let's walk through an example.

Using similar sample data as the above for sales and employee, we'll again lookup the employee's sales region:

*Sample data (the below Sales Report contains* two entries *for the same Sales Person ID)*:

## SALES REPORT:

| | A | B | C | D | E |
|---|---|---|---|---|---|
| | SALES PERSON ID | SALES PERSON FIRST | SALES PERSON LAST | REGION | Jan |
| 1 | | | | | |
| 2 | 700 | Peter | Danner | | $ 4,449 |
| 3 | 600 | Maggie | Graham | | $ 3,973 |
| 4 | 200 | Peter | Graham | | $ 1,975 |
| 5 | 400 | Helen | Simpson | | $ 7,716 |
| 6 | 300 | Alex | Steller | | $ 2,779 |
| 7 | 500 | Joe | Tanner | | $ 5,620 |
| 8 | 100 | Elizabeth | Winchester | | $ 869 |
| 9 | 300 | Butler | Catherine | | $ 1,588 |

## EMPLOYEE DATA:

| | A | B | C | D | E |
|---|---|---|---|---|---|
| 1 | SALES PERSON ID | SALES PERSON LAST | SALES PERSON FIRST | SALES REGION | MANAGER ID |
| 2 | 100 | Winchester | Elizabeth | West | 50 |
| 3 | 200 | Graham | Peter | West | 50 |
| 4 | 300 | Steller | Alex | (Central) | 30 |
| 5 | 400 | Simpson | Helen | East | 40 |
| 6 | 500 | Tanner | Joe | West | 50 |
| 7 | 600 | Graham | Maggie | Central | 30 |
| 8 | 700 | Danner | Peter | East | 40 |
| 9 | 300 | Butler | Catherine | (East) | 40 |

As the screenshot below shows, the VLOOKUP returned the value for the *first* matching **Lookup_value** it found in the **Table_array**, which in this example, is the region 'Central'.

## SALES REPORT:

D6     $f_x$   =VLOOKUP(A6,'[Employee Data.xlsx]Employee'!$A:$E,4,FALSE)

| | A | B | C | D | E | F | G | H |
|---|---|---|---|---|---|---|---|---|
| 1 | SALES PERSON ID | SALES PERSON FIRST | SALES PERSON LAST | REGION | Jan | | | |
| 2 | 700 | Peter | Danner | East | $ 4,449 | | | |
| 3 | 600 | Maggie | Graham | Central | $ 3,973 | | | |
| 4 | 200 | Peter | Graham | West | $ 1,975 | | | |
| 5 | 400 | Helen | Simpson | East | $ 7,716 | | | |
| 6 | 300 | Alex | Steller | Central | $ 2,779 | | | |
| 7 | 500 | Joe | Tanner | West | $ 5,620 | | | |
| 8 | 100 | Elizabeth | Winchester | West | $ 869 | | | |
| 9 | 300 | Butler | Catherine | Central | $ 1,588 | | | |

*Incorrect, should be the 'East' region*

Hopefully, there are system controls in place to prevent a sales person ID from being added more than once. However, I've seen situations where this can happen, especially when migrating data from another system or importing employee information due to an acquisition.

## ☑ HELPFUL INFORMATION:

To address this you could apply the **CONCAT** function to the *sales person's ID, first,* and *last name* and make that the unique **Lookup_value**. However, if you're in a position to do so, the best practice would be change the employee's sales person ID.

An easy way to identify duplicate values is to use **CONDITIONAL FORMATTING**. For example, using the employee sample data:

1. Select **column 'A'**
2. From the Ribbon select **Home**: **Conditional Formatting**
3. From the drop-down box, select the **option 'Highlight Cells Rules'** then **'Duplicate Values…'**

EMPLOYEE DATA:

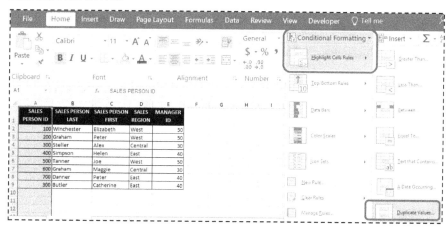

The following dialogue box should appear:

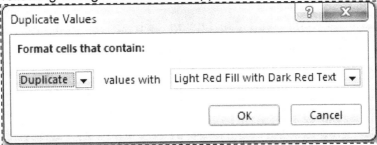

4.  Click the '**OK**' button

The following rows should now be highlighted:

| | A | B | C | D | E |
|---|---|---|---|---|---|
| 1 | SALES PERSON ID | SALES PERSON LAST | SALES PERSON FIRST | SALES REGION | MANAGER ID |
| 2 | 100 | Winchester | Elizabeth | West | 50 |
| 3 | 200 | Graham | Peter | West | 50 |
| 4 | 300 | Steller | Alex | Central | 30 |
| 5 | 400 | Simpson | Helen | East | 40 |
| 6 | 500 | Tanner | Joe | West | 50 |
| 7 | 600 | Graham | Maggie | Central | 30 |
| 8 | 700 | Danner | Peter | East | 40 |
| 9 | 300 | Butler | Catherine | East | 40 |

**To remove the Conditional Formatting:**

1.  From the Ribbon select **Home : Conditional Formatting**

2.  Select '**Clear Rules**' and either option:
    a.  Clear Rules from <u>S</u>elect Cells
    b.  Clear Rules from <u>E</u>ntire Sheet

*Please see image on next page:*

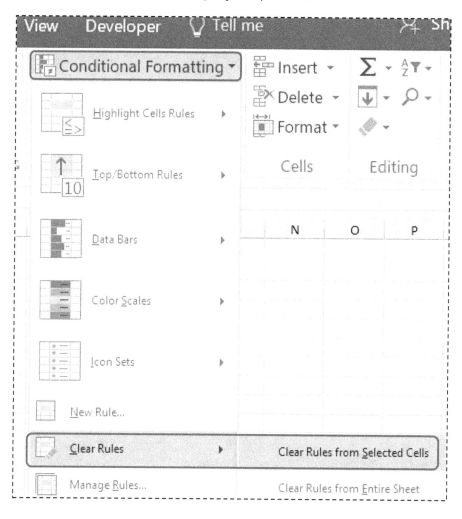

To apply the VLOOKUP formula across multiple workbooks or sheets, we will again use the **IFERROR** function, please see Chapter 3 for syntax.

**WEB ADDRESS & FILE NAMES FOR EXERCISE:**
https://bentontrainingbook.wixsite.com/bentonbooks/excel-2016
Vlookup_Example_5_ManagersReport.xlsx
Vlookup_Example_5_EmployeeData.xlsx

## Scenario:
A new sales management position has been created to oversee three sales regions. This new manager has been given a list of employee IDs, but does not know each employee's name and sales region. She has asked you to pull together all the employee data and create a consolidated **Manager's report** for her.

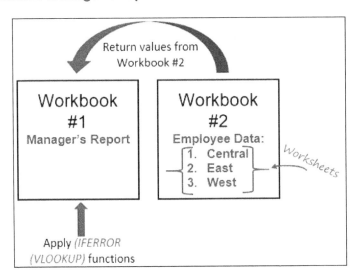

## Step-By-Step Example:

EXAMPLE 5: (APPLYING A VLOOKUP FUNCTION ACROSS
MULTIPLE WORKSHEETS & WORKBOOKS)

This exercise will require building a **nested VLOOKUP**, once completed this formula is going be very long. However, by building the **function in stages**, we will minimize errors. Also, if we run into problems it will be easier to troubleshoot, because we know the previous parts of the formula are working.

Sample data:

*Workbook #1*
*Manager's Report*

| | A | B | C | D |
|---|---|---|---|---|
| | EMPLOYEE ID | SALES PERSON LAST | SALES PERSON FIRST | SALES REGION |
| 1 | | | | |
| 2 | 100 | | | |
| 3 | 200 | | | |
| 4 | 300 | | | |
| 5 | 301 | | | |
| 6 | 400 | | | |
| 7 | 500 | | | |
| 8 | 600 | | | |
| 9 | 700 | | | |
| 10 | 702 | | | |
| 11 | | | | |

Manager's Report ⊕

Workbook #2
Employee Data, contains **3 worksheets**

| | A | B | C | D |
|---|---|---|---|---|
| 1 | EMPLOYEE ID | SALES PERSON LAST | SALES PERSON FIRST | SALES REGION |
| 2 | 300 | Steller | Alex | Central |
| 3 | 600 | Graham | Maggie | Central |
| 4 | 702 | Dockery | Kevin | Central |
| 5 | | | | |

*1*

Central | East | West | ⊕

| | A | B | C | D |
|---|---|---|---|---|
| 1 | EMPLOYEE ID | SALES PERSON LAST | SALES PERSON FIRST | SALES REGION |
| 2 | 400 | Simpson | Helen | East |
| 3 | 700 | Danner | Peter | East |
| 4 | 301 | Butler | Catherine | East |
| 5 | | | | |

*2*

Central | East | West | ⊕

| | A | B | C | D |
|---|---|---|---|---|
| 1 | EMPLOYEE ID | SALES PERSON LAST | SALES PERSON FIRST | SALES REGION |
| 2 | 100 | Winchester | Elizabeth | West |
| 3 | 200 | Graham | Peter | West |
| 4 | 500 | Tanner | Joe | West |
| 5 | | | | |

*3*

Central | East | West | ⊕

1. Open the Vlookup_Example_5_EmployeeData.xlsx spreadsheet

2.  Open the Vlookup_Example_5_ManagersReport.xlsx spreadsheet

3.  On the Vlookup_Example_5_ManagersReport.xlsx select cell '**B2**'

4.  From the Ribbon select **Formulas : Lookup & Reference**

5.  From the drop-down list, select the option '**VLOOKUP**'

6.  In the Function Arguments dialogue box enter the following:

    a.  Click cell '**A2**' or enter **A2** in the dialogue box for the '**Lookup_value**'

    b.  For '**Table_array**', click the workbook Vlookup_Example_5_EmployeeData.xlsx, the 'Central' worksheet and select columns '**A:D**'

    c.  Enter the number **2** for '**Col_index_num**'

    d.  For '**Range_lookup**' enter **False**

7.  Click the '**OK**' button

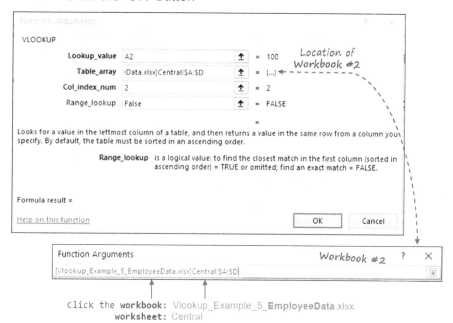

Click the **workbook**: Vlookup_Example_5_EmployeeData.xlsx
**worksheet**: Central

You'll receive the **#N/A** message, this is *OK* and to be expected. We'll address this as we go.

## Workbook #1 (Manager's Report)

8. Copy the VLOOKUP formula down to cells **'B3: B10'**, *only Rows 4, 8, & 10* should now have values:

| | A | B | C | D |
|---|---|---|---|---|
| | **EMPLOYEE ID** | **SALES PERSON LAST** | **SALES PERSON FIRST** | **SALES REGION** |
| 1 | | | | |
| 2 | 100 | #N/A | | |
| 3 | 200 | #N/A | | |
| 4 | 300 | Steller | | |
| 5 | 301 | #N/A | | |
| 6 | 400 | #N/A | | |
| 7 | 500 | #N/A | | |
| 8 | 600 | Graham | | |
| 9 | 700 | #N/A | | |
| 10 | 702 | Dockery | | |
| 11 | | | | |
| 12 | | | | |

Manager's Report ⊕

9. Next, add the **IFERROR** function to the **VLOOKUP** formula, return to cell **'B2'** and enter the following:

```
=IFERROR(VLOOKUP(A2,[Vlookup_Example_5_EmployeeData.xlsx]
    Central!$A:$D,2,FALSE),"Name Not Found")
```

10. Copy the updated IFERROR & VLOOKUP formula to cells '**B3:B10**'

**Workbook #1 (Manager's Report)**

| B2 | | | $f_x$ | =IFERROR(VLOOKUP(A2,[Vlookup_Example_5_EmployeeData.xlsx]Central! $A.$D.2,FALSE),"Name Not Found") | | | | |

| | A | B | C | D | E | F | G | H | I |
|---|---|---|---|---|---|---|---|---|---|
| 1 | EMPLOYEE ID | SALES PERSON LAST | SALES PERSON FIRST | SALES REGION | | | | | |
| 2 | 100 | Name Not Found | | | | | | | |
| 3 | 200 | Name Not Found | | | | | | | |
| 4 | 300 | Steller | | | | | | | |
| 5 | 301 | Name Not Found | | | | | | | |
| 6 | 400 | Name Not Found | | | | | | | |
| 7 | 500 | Name Not Found | | | | | | | |
| 8 | 600 | Graham | | | | | | | |
| 9 | 700 | Name Not Found | | | | | | | |
| 10 | 702 | Dockery | | | | | | | |

We've completed the first part of our nested VLOOKUP function. Next, we'll add the second element to our formula for the worksheet '**East**' region. Remember, <u>we're building our formula in stages</u>, verifying each segment works before moving on to the next step.

Unfortunately, there is no wizard for building nested functions in Excel®, therefore we'll need to augment this formula manually. In this example, *we know the remaining region worksheets are designed in the same layout as the '**Central**' region*, therefore we can copy a portion of our existing formula and modify it for the regions '**East**' and '**West**'.

11. Return to the Vlookup_Example_5_**ManagersReport**.xlsx spreadsheet and select cell '**B2**'

12. Select *(highlight)* and copy (CTRL+C) this section of the formula:
=IFERROR(VLOOKUP(A3,[Vlookup_Example_5_EmployeeData.xlsx] Central!$A:$D,2,FALSE),"Name Not Found")

13. **Paste (CTRL+V)** *before* "Name Not Found"

14. Change the text from Central! to East!

15. Add the additional parenthesis after "Name Not Found"))

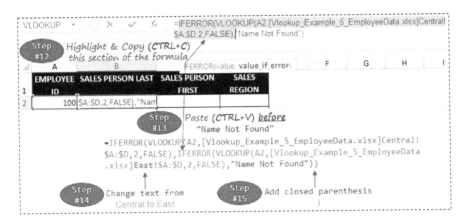

**Part 2** of the **nested Vlookup formula** should be as follows, (*there are no spaces in the below*):

```
=IFERROR(VLOOKUP(A2,[Vlookup_Example_5_EmployeeData.xlsx]
Central!$A:$D,2,FALSE),IFERROR(VLOOKUP(A2,[Vlookup_Example_
5_EmployeeData.xlsx]East!$A:$D,2,FALSE),"Name Not Found"))
```

16. Copy the updated IFERROR & VLOOKUP function to cells '**B3:B10**'

| | A | B | C | D |
|---|---|---|---|---|
| | EMPLOYEE ID | SALES PERSON LAST | SALES PERSON FIRST | SALES REGION |
| 1 | | | | |
| 2 | 100 | Name Not Found | | |
| 3 | 200 | Name Not Found | | |
| 4 | 300 | Steller | | |
| 5 | 301 | Butler | | |
| 6 | 400 | Simpson | | |
| 7 | 500 | Name Not Found | | |
| 8 | 600 | Graham | | |
| 9 | 700 | Danner | | |
| 10 | 702 | Dockery | | |

```
=IFERROR(VLOOKUP(A2,[Vlookup_Example_5_EmployeeData.xlsx]Central!$A:$D,2,FALSE),
IFERROR(VLOOKUP(A2,[Vlookup_Example_5_EmployeeData.xlsx]East!$A:$D,2,FALSE),
"Name Not Found"))
```

Almost done, next we'll add the final segment to our nested VLOOKUP function. This will search the *third worksheet* called **'West'** in Workbook #2 (Employee Data).

17. Return to the Vlookup_Example_5_**ManagersReport**.xlsx spreadsheet and select cell **'B2'**

18. Select *(highlight)* and copy (CTRL+C) this section of the formula:
    ```
    IFERROR(VLOOKUP(A2,[Vlookup_Example_5_EmployeeData.xlsx
    ]East!$A:$D,2,FALSE),"Name Not Found"))
    ```

19. **Paste (CTRL+V)** *before* "Name Not Found"))

20. Change the text from East! to West!

21. Add the additional parenthesis after "Name Not Found")))

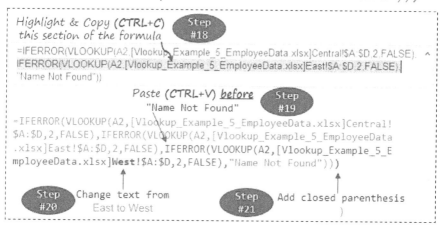

22. Copy the updated nested VLOOKUP formula to cells **'B3:B10'**

| | A | B | C | D |
|---|---|---|---|---|
| 1 | EMPLOYEE ID | SALES PERSON LAST | SALES PERSON FIRST | SALES REGION |
| 2 | 100 | Winchester | | |
| 3 | 200 | Graham | | |
| 4 | 300 | Steller | | |
| 5 | 301 | Butler | | |
| 6 | 400 | Simpson | | |
| 7 | 500 | Tanner | | |
| 8 | 600 | Graham | | |
| 9 | 700 | Danner | | |
| 10 | 702 | Dockery | | |

```
=IFERROR(VLOOKUP(A2,[Vlookup_Example_5_EmployeeData.xlsx]Central!$A:$D,2,FALSE),
IFERROR(VLOOKUP(A2,[Vlookup_Example_5_EmployeeData.xlsx]East!$A:$D,2,FALSE),
IFERROR(VLOOKUP(A2,[Vlookup_Example_5_EmployeeData.xlsx]West!$A:$D,2,FALSE),
"Name Not Found")))
```

Great job! If you had trouble, don't worry, this was a complex nested IF VLOOKUP function. You'll get better with practice. It often still takes me a couple of tries to get the formula correct and I have had years of experience. It is very easy to miss a comma or parenthesis with these advanced functions. Your skill level will improve with repetition.

To complete the scenario, we're going to copy the formula to the columns **'SALES PERSON FIRST'** & **'REGION'** on workbook #1 (Manager's Report). Before we begin copying the IFERROR & VLOOKUP function, we need to add the **U.S. dollar $** symbol to the **Lookup_value**.

23. Return to the Vlookup_Example_5_ManagersReport.xlsx spreadsheet and select cell **'B2'**

24. For each Lookup_value, add the **$ before A2**

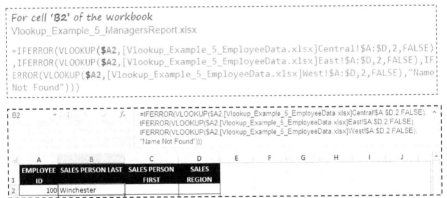

```
For cell 'B2' of the workbook
Vlookup_Example_5_ManagersReport.xlsx

=IFERROR(VLOOKUP($A2,[Vlookup_Example_5_EmployeeData.xlsx]Central!$A:$D,2,FALSE)
,IFERROR(VLOOKUP($A2,[Vlookup_Example_5_EmployeeData.xlsx]East!$A:$D,2,FALSE),IF
ERROR(VLOOKUP($A2,[Vlookup_Example_5_EmployeeData.xlsx]West!$A:$D,2,FALSE),"Name
Not Found")))
```

25. Copy the updated nested VLOOKUP formula to cell **'C2'**

26. In cell **'C2'** change the **Col_index_num** for all VLOOKUP formulas to **3**

27. Copy the updated nested VLOOKUP formula to cells **'C3:$D10'**, *please note* to copy the formula to **column 'D10'**

It is _OK_, that **column 'D'** is displaying the same values as **column 'C'**, we'll fix this in the next steps.

| | A | B | C | D |
|---|---|---|---|---|
| 1 | EMPLOYEE ID | SALES PERSON LAST | SALES PERSON FIRST | SALES REGION |
| 2 | 100 | Winchester | Elizabeth | Elizabeth |
| 3 | 200 | Graham | Peter | Peter |
| 4 | 300 | Steller | Alex | Alex |
| 5 | 301 | Butler | Catherine | Catherine |
| 6 | 400 | Simpson | Helen | Helen |
| 7 | 500 | Tanner | Joe | Joe |
| 8 | 600 | Graham | Maggie | Maggie |
| 9 | 700 | Danner | Peter | Peter |
| 10 | 702 | Dockery | Kevin | Kevin |

28. Select cell **'D2'** and change the **Col_index_num** for all VLOOKUP formulas to **4**

29. Copy the updated nested VLOOKUP formula to cells **'D3:D10'**

```
=IFERROR(VLOOKUP($A2,'[Employee Data.xlsx]Central'!$A:$D(4)FALSE),
IFERROR(VLOOKUP($A2,'[Employee Data.xlsx]East'!$A:$D(4)FALSE),
IFERROR(VLOOKUP($A2,'[Employee Data.xlsx]West'!$A:$D(4)FALSE),"Name
Not Found")))
```

| D2 | | | | *fx* | =IFERROR(VLOOKUP($A2,'[Employee Data.xlsx]Central'!$A:$D,4,FALSE), |
| | | | | | IFERROR(VLOOKUP($A2,'[Employee Data.xlsx]East'!$A:$D,4,FALSE), |
| | | | | | IFERROR(VLOOKUP($A2,'[Employee Data.xlsx]West'!$A:$D,4,FALSE),"Name |
| | | | | | Not Found"))) |

| | A | B | C | D | E | F | G | H | I |
|---|---|---|---|---|---|---|---|---|---|
| 1 | EMPLOYEE ID | SALES PERSON LAST | SALES PERSON FIRST | SALES REGION | | | | | |
| 2 | 100 | Winchester | Elizabeth | West | | | | | |
| 3 | 200 | Graham | Peter | West | | | | | |
| 4 | 300 | Steller | Alex | Central | | | | | |
| 5 | 301 | Butler | Catherine | East | | | | | |
| 6 | 400 | Simpson | Helen | East | | | | | |
| 7 | 500 | Tanner | Joe | West | | | | | |
| 8 | 600 | Graham | Maggie | Central | | | | | |
| 9 | 700 | Danner | Peter | East | | | | | |
| 10 | 702 | Dockery | Kevin | Central | | | | | |

The final report should look similar to the following:

| | A | B | C | D |
|---|---|---|---|---|
| 1 | EMPLOYEE ID | SALES PERSON LAST | SALES PERSON FIRST | SALES REGION |
| 2 | 100 | Winchester | Elizabeth | West |
| 3 | 200 | Graham | Peter | West |
| 4 | 300 | Steller | Alex | Central |
| 5 | 301 | Butler | Catherine | East |
| 6 | 400 | Simpson | Helen | East |
| 7 | 500 | Tanner | Joe | West |
| 8 | 600 | Graham | Maggie | Central |
| 9 | 700 | Danner | Peter | East |
| 10 | 702 | Dockery | Kevin | Central |

Congratulations! You've successfully applied a VLOOKUP formula across multiple worksheets and workbooks.

You've completed the scenario. The new manager has been given a consolidated report that lists the Sales Person ID, First & Last Name, and Region for all of her employees.

## EXAMPLE 6: (HOW TO USE A VLOOKUP TO LOOKUP AND CALCULATE A NUMBER BASED ON SPECIFIC CRITERIA)

In this exercise we'll review how to combine a logic formula with the Vlookup function.

**WEB ADDRESS & FILE NAME FOR EXERCISE:**
https://bentontrainingbook.wixsite.com/bentonbooks/excel-2016
Vlookup_Example_6.xlsx

## Scenario:

You've been asked to determine the following for each Sales Person:

A. If they are eligible for a bonus, based on their sales being greater than or equal to $5,000

B. If yes, what is their bonus rate, and based on that rate, calculate the dollar amount owed to them

C. If they do not qualify for a bonus, display the text **'Not Eligible'**

To accomplish this, you will use a combination of the functions **IF** & **VLOOKUP** to develop the sales report.

Sample data:

*Workbook contains 2 worksheets*

| | A | B | C |
|---|---|---|---|
| | SALES PERSON | SALES | BONUS AMOUNT? |
| 1 | | | |
| 2 | Steller, Alex | $ 6,134 | |
| 3 | Graham, Maggie | $ 4,148 | |
| 4 | Dockery, Kevin | $ 9,373 | |
| 5 | Simpson, Helen | $ 2,309 | |
| 6 | Danner, Peter | $ 2,844 | |
| 7 | Butler, Catherine | $ 3,921 | |
| 8 | Winchester, Elizabeth | $ 2,448 | |
| 9 | Graham, Peter | $ 8,708 | |
| 10 | Tanner, Joe | $ 7,995 | |
| 11 | Arnold, Mike | $ 11,052 | |

*1*
Sales Report | Bonus Rate ⊕

| | A | B | C |
|---|---|---|---|
| 1 | FROM | TO | RATE |
| 2 | $5,000 | $6,999 | 2% |
| 3 | $7,000 | $7,999 | 3% |
| 4 | $8,000 | $8,999 | 4% |
| 5 | $9,000 | $9,999 | 5% |
| 6 | | | |

*2*
Sales | Bonus Rate

PART 1 of the formula:

1. Open the Vlookup_Example_6.xlsx spreadsheet
2. Select the tab named **'Sales Report'**
3. Place your cursor in cell **'C2'**
4. From the Ribbon select **Formulas : Logical**
5. From the drop-down list, select the option **'IF'**

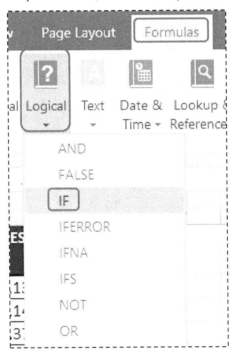

6. In the Function Arguments dialogue box enter the following:

   a. Enter **B2>=5000** in the dialogue box for the **'Logic_test'** *(this is the dollar amount to evaluate if the Sales Person is eligible for a bonus)*

   b. For **'Value_if_true'**, enter **"Y"** *(this is a temporary value, to verify the first part of the formula is working, this will eventually be replaced with the Vlookup function)*

   c. For **'Value_if_false'**, enter **"Not Eligible"** *(text to display if the Sales Person sales were $4,999 or less)*

7. Click the **'OK'** button

Function Arguments

IF

| | | | | |
|---|---|---|---|---|
| Logical_test | B2>=5000 | ↑ | = | TRUE |
| Value_if_true | "Y" | ↑ | = | "Y" |
| Value_if_false | "Not Eligible" | ↑ | = | "Not Eligible" |

= "Y"

Checks whether a condition is met, and returns one value if TRUE, and another value if FALSE.

**Value_if_false** is the value that is returned if Logical_test is FALSE. If omitted, FALSE is returned.

Formula result = Y

Help on this function    OK    Cancel

8. Copy this formula to cells **'C3:C11'**

The following should now be displayed. We've verified the first stage of the formula is working correctly:

C2    $f_x$    =IF(B2>=5000,"Y","Not Eligible")

| | A | B | C | D | E |
|---|---|---|---|---|---|
| 1 | SALES PERSON | SALES | BONUS AMOUNT? | | |
| 2 | Steller, Alex | $ 6,134 | Y | | |
| 3 | Graham, Maggie | $ 4,148 | Not Eligible | | |
| 4 | Dockery, Kevin | $ 9,373 | Y | | |
| 5 | Simpson, Helen | $ 2,309 | Not Eligible | | |
| 6 | Danner, Peter | $ 2,844 | Not Eligible | | |
| 7 | Butler, Catherine | $ 3,921 | Not Eligible | | |
| 8 | Winchester, Elizabeth | $ 2,448 | Not Eligible | | |
| 9 | Graham, Peter | $ 8,708 | Y | | |
| 10 | Tanner, Joe | $ 7,995 | Y | | |
| 11 | Arnold, Mike | $ 11,052 | Y | | |

## PART 2 of the formula:

9. Select cell **'C2'**

10. Highlight the **'Value_if_true'**, **"Y"** and from the Ribbon select **Formulas : Lookup & Reference**

C·J· Benton

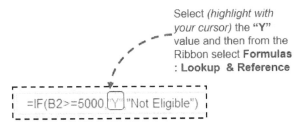

Select *(highlight with your cursor)* the **"Y"** value and then from the Ribbon select **Formulas** : **Lookup & Reference**

=IF(B2>=5000,Y,"Not Eligible")

11. From the drop-down list, select the option **'VLOOKUP'**

12. In the Function Arguments dialogue box enter the following:

    a. Click cell **'B2'** or enter **B2** in the dialogue box for the **'Lookup_value'** *(the sales number to evaluate)*

    b. For **'Table_array'**, click on the tab **'Bonus Rate'** and select columns **'A:C'** *(this is the range of cells we're searching)*

    c. Enter the number **3** for **'Col_index_num'** *(this column contains the bonus rate)*

    d. For **'Range_lookup'** enter **True** *(to return an approximate match)*

13. Click the **'OK'** button

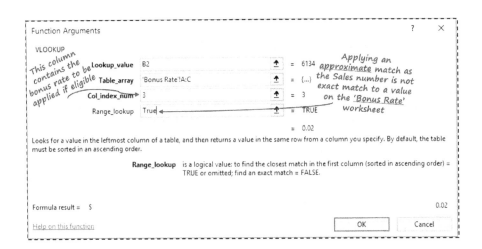

The following should now be displayed, we've verified 2% is the correct multiplier for the bonus rate for sales greater than $5,000, but less than $7,000:

| C2 | | | $f_x$ | =IF(B2>=5000,VLOOKUP(B2,'Bonus Rate'!A:C,3,TRUE),"Not Eligible") | | | | |
|---|---|---|---|---|---|---|---|---|
| | A | B | C | D | E | F | G | H |
| 1 | SALES PERSON | SALES | BONUS AMOUNT? | | | | | |
| 2 | Steller, Alex | $ 6,134 | $ 0.02 | | | | | |
| 3 | Graham, Maggie | $ 4,148 | Not Eligible | | | | | |

=IF(B2>=5000,**VLOOKUP(B2,'Bonus Rate'!A:C,3,TRUE)**,"Not Eligible")

## PART 3 of the formula:

14. To calculate the dollar amount owed to the sales person if eligible, place your cursor in cell '**C2**'

15. Modify the formula as follows:

=IF(B2>=5000,**(**VLOOKUP(B2,'Bonus Rate'!A:C,3,TRUE)**\*B2)**,"Not Eligible")

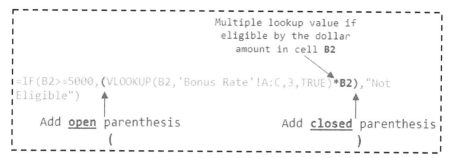

16. Copy this formula to cells '**C3:C11**'

The following should now be displayed, we've completed the sales report per the requirements requested:

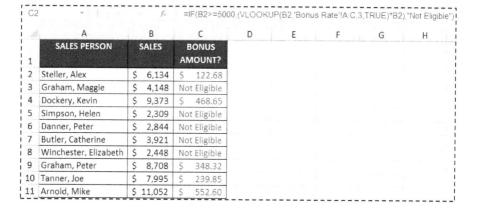

| C2 | | | $f_x$ | =IF(B2>=5000,(VLOOKUP(B2,'Bonus Rate'!A:C,3,TRUE)*B2),"Not Eligible") | | | | |
|---|---|---|---|---|---|---|---|---|
| | A | B | C | D | E | F | G | H |
| 1 | SALES PERSON | SALES | BONUS AMOUNT? | | | | | |
| 2 | Steller, Alex | $ 6,134 | $ 122.68 | | | | | |
| 3 | Graham, Maggie | $ 4,148 | Not Eligible | | | | | |
| 4 | Dockery, Kevin | $ 9,373 | $ 468.65 | | | | | |
| 5 | Simpson, Helen | $ 2,309 | Not Eligible | | | | | |
| 6 | Danner, Peter | $ 2,844 | Not Eligible | | | | | |
| 7 | Butler, Catherine | $ 3,921 | Not Eligible | | | | | |
| 8 | Winchester, Elizabeth | $ 2,448 | Not Eligible | | | | | |
| 9 | Graham, Peter | $ 8,708 | $ 348.32 | | | | | |
| 10 | Tanner, Joe | $ 7,995 | $ 239.85 | | | | | |
| 11 | Arnold, Mike | $ 11,052 | $ 552.60 | | | | | |

While the VLOOKUP and associated functions are very useful and quite powerful, it can be challenging and sometimes frustrating to learn them. Why a VLOOKUP is not returning the correct value can puzzle even the most experienced users. The final chapter in this book addresses some of the more common VLOOKUP errors and how to resolve them. The areas reviewed are:

- Why I am receiving the **#N/A error message**?
- My **Lookup_value** is the same as the match value in the **Table_array**, why is my VLOOKUP formula not returning a value?
- Why am I getting the **#REF error message**?
- My VLOOKUP formula was working, but now I'm getting the wrong values, why?

Some of the below examples can be a little tricky to understand as they involve formatting issues, such as extra spaces and/or mis-matched text case of the Lookup_value. However, with a little practice knowing what to look for and how to resolve these issues you will save yourself hours of aggravation!

## #N/A ERROR MESSAGE (EXAMPLE 1)

| ERROR | Why I am receiving the **#N/A error message**? |
|---|---|
| POSSIBLE EXPLANATION | The field you want to match, the **Lookup_value**, *IS NOT* the *FIRST COLUMN* in the range of cells you specify in the **Table_array** |
| EXAMPLE | VLOOKUP formula appears correct, but since we're matching on the **'SALES PERSON ID'**, this column needs to be *FIRST* in the Table_array. |

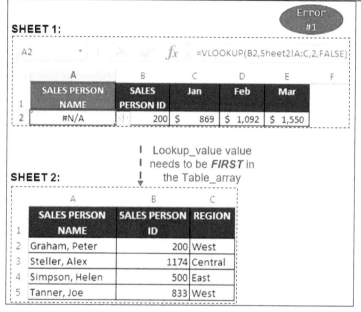

| SOLUTION | Make the **'SALES PERSON ID'**, the first column in the Table_array. |
|---|---|

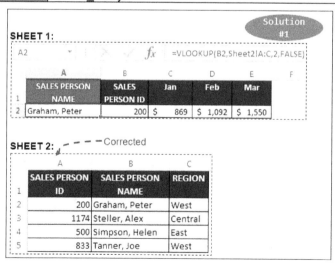

## #N/A ERROR MESSAGE (EXAMPLE 2)

| ERROR | Why I am getting the **#N/A error message**? My **Lookup_value** _is_ the FIRST COLUMN in the range of cells specified in the Table_array. What else could be wrong? |
|---|---|
| POSSIBLE EXPLANATION | **Extra spaces** in the Lookup_value or Table_array |
| EXAMPLE | Most of the time you can't see extra spaces, especially if they are after the Lookup_value, but these invisible nuisances will cause your VLOOKUP to fail. |

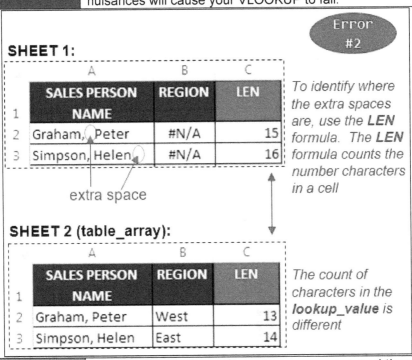

| SOLUTION | Identify if and where the extra spaces are and then remove them |
|---|---|

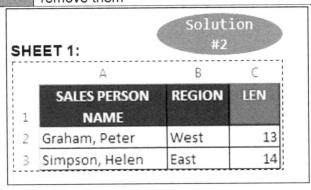

## #N/A ERROR MESSAGE (EXAMPLE 3)

| ERROR | What else could cause the **#N/A error message** |
|---|---|
| POSSIBLE EXPLANATION | A similar formatting issue causing a VLOOKUP to fail is related to *__mismatched case__* of the Lookup_value. |

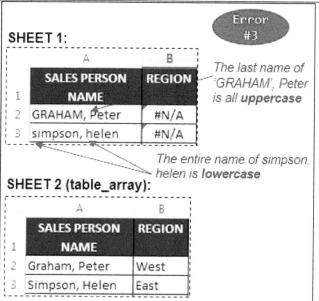

| SOLUTION | Change the case formatting to match the Table_array |
|---|---|

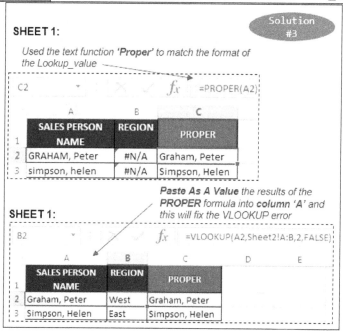

#REF ERROR MESSAGE

| ERROR | Why am I getting the **#REF** error message? |
|---|---|
| **POSSIBLE EXPLANATION** | A common cause is the **Table_array** range of cells is incorrect. |

In the example below, the VLOOKUP in sheet 1 is referencing *2 columns* in the Table_array. The **#REF error** is because the **Col_index_num** is referencing *column 3*, but that column is NOT included in the Table_array.

**SHEET 1:**

| C2 | | | | | *fx* | =VLOOKUP($A2,Sheet2!$A:$B,3,FALSE) |

| | A | B | C | D | E | F |
|---|---|---|---|---|---|---|
| 1 | **SALES PERSON NAME** | **REGION** | **MANAGER ID** | | | |
| 2 | Graham, Peter | We: | #REF! | | | |
| 3 | Simpson, Helen | East | #REF! | | | |

**SHEET 2 (Table_array):**

| | A | B | C |
|---|---|---|---|
| 1 | Number of Columns: | | |
| 2 | **1** | **2** | **3** |
| 3 | **SALES PERSON NAME** | **REGION** | **MANAGER ID** |
| 4 | Graham, Peter | West | 50 |
| 5 | Simpson, Helen | East | 40 |

| SOLUTION | Change the Table_array to include the correct number of columns. |
|---|---|

**SHEET 1:**

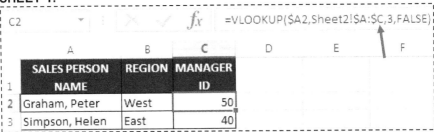

| C2 | | | | | *fx* | =VLOOKUP($A2,Sheet2!$A:$C,3,FALSE) |

| | A | B | C | D | E | F |
|---|---|---|---|---|---|---|
| 1 | **SALES PERSON NAME** | **REGION** | **MANAGER ID** | | | |
| 2 | Graham, Peter | West | 50 | | | |
| 3 | Simpson, Helen | East | 40 | | | |

## MY VLOOKUP FORMULA WAS WORKING, BUT NOW I'M GETTING THE WRONG VALUES, WHY?

### ERROR / ISSUE:

| ERROR | Why did my Vlookup stop working? |
|---|---|
| POSSIBLE EXPLANATION | Someone has inadvertently added or deleted columns in the **Table_array** range of cells |

In the example below, REGION *was* being populated correctly. Let's say, you reviewed this report on a Friday, but then on the following Monday, when you opened the same report, the results were different. Why?

**SHEET 1** (correct on *Friday*):

| | A | B | C |
|---|---|---|---|
| | SALES PERSON NAME | REGION | MANAGER ID |
| 1 | | | |
| 2 | Graham, Peter | West | 50 |
| 3 | Simpson, Helen | East | 40 |

**SHEET 1** (incorrect on *Monday*):

| | A | B | C |
|---|---|---|---|
| | SALES PERSON NAME | REGION | MANAGER ID |
| 1 | | | |
| 2 | Graham, Peter | 100 | West |
| 3 | Simpson, Helen | 200 | East |

After reviewing the Table_array, you discover someone has added **two new columns**; 'SALES PERSON ID' and 'HOME OFFICE LOCATION'.

### SHEET 2 (Table_array):

| | A | B | C | D | E |
|---|---|---|---|---|---|
| | SALES PERSON NAME | SALES PERSON ID | HOME OFFICE LOCATION | REGION | MANAGER ID |
| 1 | | | | | |
| 2 | Graham, Peter | 100 | Seattle | West | 50 |
| 3 | Simpson, Helen | 200 | London | East | 40 |

| SOLUTION | Adjust your VLOOKUP formula to account for the newly inserted columns. |
|---|---|

### SHEET 1:

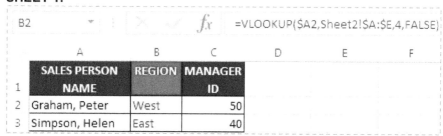

| B2 | | | | *fx* | =VLOOKUP($A2,Sheet2!$A:$E,4,FALSE) |

| | A | B | C | D | E | F |
|---|---|---|---|---|---|---|
| | SALES PERSON NAME | REGION | MANAGER ID | | | |
| 1 | | | | | | |
| 2 | Graham, Peter | West | 50 | | | |
| 3 | Simpson, Helen | East | 40 | | | |

**Thank you** for purchasing and reading this book! Your feedback is valued and appreciated! Please take a few minutes and leave a review.

1. Microsoft® Excel® **Start Here The Beginners Guide**

2. The Step-By-Step Guide To The **25 Most Common Microsoft® Excel® Formulas & Features** *(version 2013)*

3. The Excel® 2016 **The 30 Most Common Formulas & Features** - The Step-By-Step Guide *(version 2016)*

4. The Step-By-Step Guide To **Pivot Tables & Introduction To Dashboards** *(version 2013)*

5. **Excel® Pivot Tables & Introduction To Dashboards** The Step-By-Step Guide *(version 2016)*

6. The Step-By-Step Guide To The **VLOOKUP** formula in Microsoft® Excel® *(version 2013)*

7. The Microsoft® Excel® Step-By-Step Training Guide **Book Bundle** *(version 2013)*

8. **Excel® Macros & VBA For Business Users** - A Beginners Guide

9. **Microsoft® Word® Essentials** The Step-By-Step Guide

www.ingramcontent.com/pod-product-compliance
Lightning Source LLC
LaVergne TN
LVHW012334060326
832902LV00011B/1875